Wage Levels and Inequality

Measuring and Interpreting the Trends

Marvin H. Kosters

D1739018

The AEI Press

Publisher for the American Enterprise Institute

WASHINGTON, D.C.

1998

I thank Randolph Stempski for his work assembling the data, and Kenneth Brown, Ed Dale, and Murray Foss for helpful comments on an earlier draft.

Available in the United States from the AEI Press, c/o Publisher Resources Inc., 1224 Heil Quaker Blvd., P.O. Box 7001, La Vergne, TN 37086-7001. To order, call toll free 1-800-269-6267. Distributed outside the United States by arrangement with Eurospan, 3 Henrietta Street, London WC2E 8LU, England.

ISBN 0-8447-7122-8

1 3 5 7 9 10 8 6 4 2

THE AEI PRESS
Publisher for the American Enterprise Institute
1150 17th Street, N.W., Washington, D.C. 20036

Printed in the United States of America

Contents

Foreword

This study is one of a series commissioned by the American Enterprise Institute on trends in the level and distribution of U.S. wages, income, wealth, consumption, and other measures of material welfare. The issues addressed in the series involve much more than dry statistics: they touch on fundamental aspirations of the American people—material progress, widely shared prosperity, and just reward for individual effort—and affect popular understanding of the successes and shortcomings of the private market economy and of particular government policies. For these reasons, discussions of "economic inequality" in the media and political debate are often partial and partisan as well as superficial. The AEI series is intended to improve the public discussion by bringing new data to light, exploring the strengths and weaknesses of various measures of economic welfare, and highlighting important questions of interpretation, causation, and consequence.

Each study in the series is presented and discussed in draft form at an AEI seminar before publication by the AEI Press. Marvin Kosters, director of economic policy studies at AEI, organized the series and moderated the seminars. A current list of published studies appears on the last page.

CHRISTOPHER DEMUTH
President
American Enterprise Institute
for Public Policy Research

1

Introduction

This volume addresses two questions: First, what has happened to the *level* of real wages during the past two or three decades? Second, what has happened to wage *inequality,* and how should we interpret changes in the *distribution* of wages? Both questions have received a great deal of popular discussion, but the changes that took place over that period and their significance have often been distorted or exaggerated. Indeed, the performance of the economy as a whole is often described in somewhat contradictory ways.

One prominent perspective on the American economy celebrates its extraordinarily good performance. Output has grown rapidly. Payrolls are up strongly, welfare rolls are down, and measures of consumer confidence are high. Profits are healthy, and the stock market has risen increasingly rapidly to new highs. Unanticipated increases in tax revenues have been shrinking the federal budget deficit. Unemployment and inflation are low, and they have stayed at levels lower than previously seemed feasible. In summary, on the basis of those measures, U.S. economic performance in the late 1990s is impressive in its own right, and it looks even better in comparison with that of other industrial countries.

Another perspective suggests that workers are anxious and insecure about their jobs in view of widespread downsizing by well-known firms. Many workers can get only part-time or temporary jobs, according to that view, and real wages of the average worker have declined. The vast majority of workers are usually said to be losing ground, with young and less-skilled workers experiencing reductions in real wages that are especially pronounced. In addition to stagnation or decline in real wage levels, a growing gap between wages of the workers with low earnings and those who are better off is often described as a serious threat to social harmony. The main emphasis from that perspective is on how poorly the typical worker has fared and on a growing gap between those who need to struggle to achieve a middle-class income and the few rich households that have claimed all the gains.

Juxtaposition of those two contradictory perspectives seems to suggest that the extraordinarily good performance of the economy has not improved the economic circumstances of most of the work force. And this is in fact what some commentaries on the economy suggest. Laura Tyson, one of President Clinton's chief economic advisers during his first term, began an article as follows:

> During the past four years, the American economy has enjoyed a robust expansion with low unemployment, greater international competitiveness and modest inflation. Unfortunately, the economy's expansion has failed to reverse two disturbing long-run trends: stagnant or falling real earnings for the majority of workers and increasing income inequality among workers and households.[1]

In that, and in many other articles, characterizing the economy in such a way serves as a preamble to developing arguments about what should be at the forefront of our policy agenda.

Analysts have widely recognized the slowdown in real wage growth since the 1950s and 1960s and the increase in wage inequality that began in the 1970s. Strong differences of opinion exist, however, about the most important causes of those trends, their social and economic consequences, and the most promising policies to counter them.

Equally important, despite the many descriptive studies that have documented changes in workers' economic circumstances, are the disputes about facts that purport to show how much better or worse off workers have become over the years. Chapter 2 of this volume reviews the most important basic data used to describe trends in the average worker's pay, with an emphasis on making distinctions that are necessary to construct a realistic picture of changes in workers' economic status.

My analysis indicates that the economic circumstances of the average worker have not deteriorated during the past twenty-five years. Instead, the average worker has fared much better than many commentators have suggested on the basis of widely cited earnings data that are incomplete and misleading. Although wage dispersion has widened since the late 1970s, much of that increased dispersion represents a recovery of educational wage premiums from levels that were temporarily depressed in the 1970s to the more normal levels that prevailed in the 1980s. The rise in the wage premium for education has stimulated youth to acquire more schooling, but despite that increase in wage inequality, wages of workers in different schooling categories still occupy much common ground.

2

Real Pay of the Average Worker

I t is easy to assemble data that appear to support quite different impressions about what has happened to economic well-being. The data shown in figure 2–1, for example, appear to indicate dramatic deterioration in the average worker's earnings and stagnant family income. According to those data, average weekly earnings, after adjustment for inflation, have declined erratically for about twenty-five years. The decline has been so pronounced that the average worker earns less in the 1990s than at any time since the late 1950s. Thus, those data suggest that the typical worker is back to where he was forty years ago. Family income, as it is reported in figure 2–1, has shown essentially no trend for the past twenty-five years, although it has moved up and down with changes in the economy. Those data seem to describe a situation in which more people need to work to maintain family income: people apparently need to work harder just to stay even.

Other data, such as those charted in figure 2–2, suggest a more optimistic picture. According to those data, the average worker's total hourly compensation has continued growing, albeit at a slower pace since the mid-1970s. In addition, the amount of total output per person in the population has increased substantially more rapidly than compensation. In contrast to a decline in real average

FIGURE 2–1
REAL MEDIAN FAMILY INCOME, 1947–1996, AND AVERAGE WEEKLY EARNINGS OF PRODUCTION AND NONSUPERVISORY WORKERS, 1947–1997
(1996 dollars)

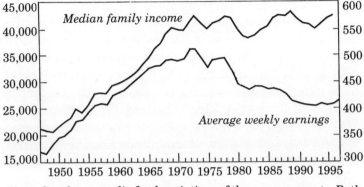

NOTE: See the appendix for descriptions of the measurements. Both measures are adjusted for inflation using the consumer price index (CPI-U).
SOURCE: Bureau of Labor Statistics and Bureau of the Census.

FIGURE 2–2
REAL PER CAPITA GDP AND INDEX OF REAL COMPENSATION PER HOUR, 1947–1997
(1997 dollars)

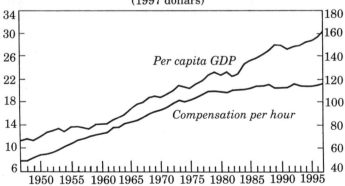

NOTE: See the appendix for descriptions of the measurements. The compensation data are adjusted for inflation using CPI-U-X1. Real per capita GDP is adjusted for inflation using the chained GDP deflator.
SOURCE: Bureau of Labor Statistics; Bureau of Economic Analysis; and Bureau of the Census.

weekly earnings of about 10 percent since the mid-1960s, real per capita gross domestic output has increased by about 80 percent. Figures 2–1and 2–2 show how analysts can assemble data of different kinds to create a picture of either serious economic deterioration or widespread economic improvement.

We need not digress at this point to discuss all the reasons for the different patterns shown by the data in those two figures or to try to reconcile them. It is probably sufficient to note that the data in the two figures come from different basic sources, the concepts they measure are quite different, and analysts used different measures of price change to adjust for inflation.[2] In the chapter that follows, I examine some of the distinctions relevant for assessing what has happened to workers' pay.

Real Wage Levels

Description of real wage levels for most workers as "stagnant" or "falling" is quite typical in discussions about how workers have fared.[3] General statements along those lines are frequently supplemented by reference to particular wage measures or segments of the work force that sharpen an impression of widespread deterioration in workers' economic well-being. In her article, for example, Laura Tyson emphasized her point by making reference to "the powerful and diverse forces driving inequality and the economic disaster that has befallen low-skilled workers, especially young men, in recent years."[4] Commentators first describe the average worker as falling behind and then underscore the point with information on a demographic group that has fared worst in recent years.

In his widely cited book, *The Future of Capitalism,* Lester Thurow said that "the real hourly wages of nonsupervisory workers (those who do not boss anyone else—a vast majority of the workforce) declined 14 percent" from 1973 to 1995.[5] In another context, he is quoted as saying that "it is really true that it now takes a mother and father working to make approximately the same amount of money that the father by himself used to make if you're in the bottom 40 percent of the population."[6] Popular discussion usually treats the idea that workers have fallen behind in economic terms as a widely accepted fact.

Characterizations of workers as falling behind are not confined to polemical discussions of the economy. A report on the fiscal outlook for higher education sponsored by the Commission on National Investment in Higher Education and published by a unit of the RAND Corporation, for example, noted that "workers right in the middle of the distribution . . . have lost about 14 percent in real wages" over the past twenty years. If present trends continue, according to the report, by 2015 workers near the median "will be earning about 25 percent less than they earned in 1976," and workers in the bottom 10 percent "will be earning a little more than half of what they earned in 1976."[7]

Statements of that kind present a bleak picture of how the typical worker has fared, the even poorer circumstances of younger and less-skilled workers, and the economic prospects facing workers in the years ahead. Those various statements about how far workers have fallen behind during the past twenty years or more all appeal to data that, at a superficial level at least, lend support to such unfavorable assessments. The scope and magnitude of the alleged deterioration in economic well-being of so many in the work force raise questions about the extent to which the wage measures cited are consistent with other measures that show economic improvement. Accurate diagnosis of the cause of a problem is often said to be an essential precondition for prescribing a solution. But before trying to diagnose a cause, we need a realistic assessment of the nature and magnitude of the problem. To make a contribution to a more realistic description of how workers have fared, I start with an examination of wage and compensation measures to piece together information on how pay levels have changed over time.

Measures of Workers' Pay

To assess what has happened to workers' real rewards for work, we must pay close attention to distinctions between different measures of pay. The data charted in figure 2–3 illustrate the importance of making such distinctions. Both series in that figure—average compensation per hour and average hourly earnings—are measures that appear to describe how the typical worker has fared. But the story they tell about what happened to workers' pay is quite different, particularly after 1973. According to those data, real average compensation per hour of work increased by about 16 percent since 1973, while real average hourly earnings declined by almost 9 percent—a twenty-five percentage point difference.[8]

Average hourly earnings are so widely used as a measure of how workers have been faring that it is important to look at that measure in some detail.[9] Careful examination of average hourly earnings is important because that measure of wages has a number of limitations and shortcomings that lead to serious understatement of cumulative increases in the typical worker's pay. To explain some of the limitations of earnings as a measure of workers' pay, I shall first compare it with the more comprehensive measure, compensation per hour.

Differences in the behavior of those two measures of workers' pay are attributable to differences in both the pay concept that they are designed to measure and the workers whose pay they are intended to represent. The average hourly earnings series covers only part of the workers who are included in the hourly compensation series. Neither measure includes agricultural or government workers, but the industry sectors they cover are fairly comparable. Within industry sectors, however, the average

FIGURE 2–3
REAL AVERAGE HOURLY EARNINGS AND COMPENSATION,
1947–1997
(Index: 1973 = 100)

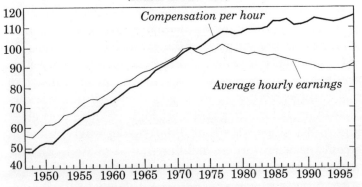

NOTE: See the appendix for descriptions of the measurements. Both measures are adjusted for inflation using CPI-U-X1.
SOURCE: Bureau of Labor Statistics.

hourly earnings series includes only production and nonsupervisory workers—mainly workers whose managerial responsibilities are fairly limited. Workers in that production and nonsupervisory category account for about 80 percent of total employment in private nonfarm industries. Those production and nonsupervisory workers, whose wages are reflected in the average hourly earnings data, account for about 65 percent of total employment in the economy.

Average hourly earnings also include only part of workers' pay. Nonwage benefits, such as the portions of the cost of health plans and pension contributions that employers pay, are excluded. In addition, the average hourly earnings measure includes only part of cash wage payments to workers. Cash payments that are not made on a regular basis, such as year-end bonuses or profit-sharing payments, are not included in that measure. Those and other limitations of the average hourly earnings measure, which I shall describe in more detail, result in much smaller cumulative increases in average hourly earnings than for compensation per hour.

In addition to covering only part of total compensation for only part of the work force, the part of the work force that is covered by the average hourly earnings measure is not representative of the work force as a whole. In particular, only production and nonsupervisory workers are included—workers with somewhat lower skills than the average worker—and wages of less-skilled workers have fallen behind wages of more highly skilled workers.[10] Figure 2–4 illustrates that difference in wage trends in recent years for workers in different, but related, skill categories. A great deal of overlap exists between hourly workers—workers who report that they are paid by the hour—and production and nonsupervisory workers, with workers paid by the hour apparently making up a majority of those workers. As the figure shows, hourly workers receive lower wages than salaried workers do, and their wages have declined relative to wages of salaried workers. In view of the decline in the relative pay of less-skilled workers, a measure like average hourly earnings that does not include the more highly paid managerial workers would increase less (or decline more) than a measure of wages that includes those workers. A measure that includes managerial workers would be more representative of the work force as a whole.

The best-known component of workers' pay included in compensation per hour but not in average hourly earnings is nonwage benefits. Wage payments that are included in average hourly earnings account for about 80 percent of total compensation. Nonwage benefits—or "fringe" benefits—include mainly payments that employers make to provide their employees with health plans, employers' contributions for Social Security, and payments they make to fund private pension plans.[11] The costs of payments of that kind have increased more rapidly than wage costs: total wage payments in current dollars have gone up by a fac-

FIGURE 2–4
Real Median Hourly Earnings for Hourly and Salaried Employees, 1978–1996
(1995 dollars)

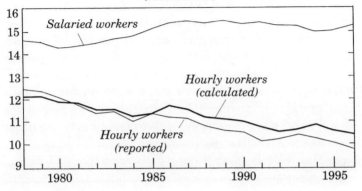

NOTE: See the appendix for descriptions of the measurements. Reported hourly earnings for hourly workers are self-reported. Medians are deflated by CPI-U-X1.
SOURCE: Bureau of the Census and Bureau of Labor Statistics.

tor of about six during the past twenty-five years, while employer payments for benefits have gone up by a factor of more than nine. That is one reason why the more comprehensive measure—compensation per hour—has increased more rapidly over the years than average hourly earnings, which include only wage payments.

A less commonly known feature of average hourly earnings that makes it an incomplete measure is that it does not include even all wage payments that are made in cash. Average hourly earnings include only earnings that show up in the payroll as regular wage payments. Wage payments made irregularly as bonuses or profit sharing are excluded. Comprehensive data on the importance of irregular wage payments are not available, but wage payments in that form are apparently not negligible. Data on union wage contracts, for example, show that those contracts provide for irregular wage payments for 40 to 45 percent of workers covered by such agreements.[12] The size of some of those bonus payments has sometimes been substantial, as illustrated by profit-sharing payments made to employees of automobile companies and often amount to several thousand dollars per worker.[13] Although data that are available from periodic surveys of compensation practices may not be representative, they indicate that wage payments in that form are not limited to workers under union contracts. Because average hourly earnings do not include irregular wage payments, that measure of wage payments understates what workers are actually paid; and if such payments have increased as a proportion of workers' pay, measures of average hourly earnings growth are understating the increase of total pay.

The validity of average hourly earnings as a cumulative measure of how workers have fared is also limited because those data are never benchmarked. That is, although the employment component of those data is adjusted regularly to incorporate additional information that becomes available about actual employment levels, the average hourly earnings data are not.[14] For example, average hourly earnings reflect no information on earnings of employees of newly established firms. The effect of those circumstances on average hourly earnings is not known. Average hourly earnings, however, are only a partial measure of workers' pay because nonwage benefits and some kinds of cash wage payments are not included, and average hourly earnings are particularly deficient as a measure of cumulative pay gains if some of those missing components of pay are growing as a proportion of the total.

Who Are Production and Nonsupervisory Workers?

A shift in the characteristics of workers included in the production and nonsupervisory worker category is a subtler source of the slump in average hourly earnings for those workers. The decline in average hourly earnings after the mid-1970s is partly a consequence of a change in the mixture of workers whose wages are being measured instead of a change in the wages of a representative group of workers. The source of that change in mixture is interesting, and its effects are ironic.

One of the first actions of the Reagan administration after it took office in January 1981 was to freeze and postpone indefinitely the last-minute "midnight regulations" published by the Carter administration to give the new administration a chance to review their merit. One of those regulations involved a badly needed update of the wage cutoff used to help classify workers for purposes of the Fair Labor Standards Act—that is, for making a distinction that many firms apparently use to report on their "production and nonsupervisory" workers.[15] Like the other midnight regulations, it was stopped in its tracks. The consequences of that little-noticed event for wage measurement have received scant attention.

As it happens, once employers have broken down their work force for the purpose of administering the minimum wage and overtime provisions of the Fair Labor Standards Act, they apparently often use the same breakdown for statistical reporting on wages and hours to the Bureau of Labor Statistics, especially in the service industries.[16] Because of rapid inflation in the late 1970s, the wage cutoff used to help define production and nonsupervisory workers—which was set in nominal terms—became increasingly out of date and artificially low. The declining wage cutoff meant that more and more workers with middle-to-higher wages were not being classified as production workers and were thus being excluded from the workers whose wages were being reported for statistical purposes. In other words, when the dividing line keeps sinking, even if no worker's wage was actually changed, the average wage—as it is measured—would decline. As a result, the reported average hourly wage of production and nonsupervisory workers would be depressed.

The Carter administration recognized that an update in that regulatory wage test was needed, but the update was proposed so late that it was caught in the new administration's freeze. Moreover, the indefinite postponement turned out to be truly indefinite; an update has still not occurred.[17]

The result has almost certainly been to distort, in a downward direction, the statistics on average hourly earnings of production and nonsupervisory workers that have been so crucial in the argument of those who have claimed that the real wages of the "typical" worker have declined. The great irony is that the Reagan administration itself unintentionally caused a statistical distortion in the underlying data that commentators frequently cited as evidence of failure of the Reagan administration's economic policies.

The criteria established by regulations to distinguish between workers exempt from the minimum wage and overtime provisions of the Fair Labor Standards Act and nonexempt employees are complicated, but they boil down to a duties test and a wage test.[18] The regulations set a wage level necessary to qualify as an exempt employee, provided that detailed primary supervisory duties tests are met. The higher the wage level needed to meet the wage test, the fewer workers could be classified as exempt and the more workers would be included in reports on production and nonsupervisory workers.

The critical point for measurement of average hourly earnings is that the regulatory wage test level is set in nominal terms, and it has not been revised since 1975. Figure 2–5 charts the level of the real regulatory test wage and average hourly earnings. (Both measures are adjusted for inflation by using the same price index and are charted in 1975 dollars.) Inflation and productivity growth have escalated the entire wage distribution since the mid-1970s. Nominal average hourly earnings are more than two and a half times higher now than they were then.

The regulations set the minimum long-test wage at a level equivalent to $3.88 per hour in 1975 for most occu-

FIGURE 2–5
REAL AVERAGE HOURLY EARNINGS AND REGULATORY TEST WAGE
FOR EXEMPT STATUS, 1950–1997
(1975 dollars)

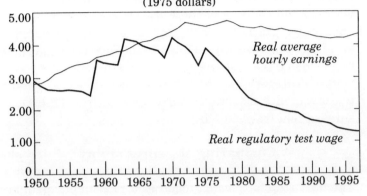

NOTE: See the appendix for descriptions of the measurements. Both
measures are adjusted for inflation using CPI-U-X1.
SOURCE: Bureau of Labor Statistics.

pations, at a time when hourly earnings averaged $4.53
and the federal minimum wage was $2.10. The nominal
wage test is far lower now in relation to the current nominal level of average hourly earnings of over $12.50 and
well below the $5.15 federal minimum wage. The persis-
tent decline in the real level of the test wage after the
mid-1970s that is shown in figure 2–5 reflects its cumulative erosion.

The main test that a worker needs to meet to be classified as an exempt employee, of course, involves duties—
whether the job entails exercise of discretion and supervisory responsibilities. But regulatory wage levels were also
apparently relevant for implementing the test during the
1970s, before the erosion in the real level of the wage test
lowered the threshold for exemption to the point where
the wage test became irrelevant.[19] Preventing the upward
adjustment in the wage test from going into effect in 1981
forced the real level of the wage test to decline to a much

lower position in the wage distribution and allowed increasing numbers of workers to qualify as exempt on the basis of their wage level. Although the dividing line is not the same as that between production and nonsupervisory workers and the rest of the work force, many employers apparently use it for their reports on employment and earnings. The resulting change in the mixture of workers included in reports on the production-and-nonsupervisory-workers category may help account for the wide cumulative divergence of average hourly earnings from other measures of real wage trends.

Comparing Measures of Pay

The next step for piecing together a reasonable estimate of what has happened to the pay of the average worker draws on comparisons of measures from four different underlying data sources. The data used to construct the measure of wages called "average hourly earnings of production and nonsupervisory workers" come from a monthly survey of employers, often referred to as the Current Employment Survey program. I label that measure as "average hourly earnings (ES)" for the origins of the data from an employers' survey.[20]

    The source of data for average compensation per hour is information from employers that is based on quarterly reports they file when they make tax payments to comply with state unemployment insurance laws. Although data from other sources are also used to construct those measures, the wage and salary totals are derived from those reports. Those data are used to construct the National Income and Product Accounts (to measure national income and gross domestic product, for example), and the data are periodically revised, updated, and benchmarked. I label data from that source as "compensation (NA)" and "wages and salaries (NA)" for their National Accounts origin.[21] The measures charted in figure 2–3, for example, are based on those first two underlying data sources.

The source of data for another measure of both compensation and wages and salaries is the Employment Cost Index (ECI) program. The Bureau of Labor Statistics uses regular periodic surveys to collect data from employers on the pay that workers receive for many detailed occupations and job descriptions.[22] One of the important strengths of those data is that they include information on both wages and nonwage benefits. One of the most important limitations of those data is that, although data on wages and salaries extend back a few years earlier, data on nonwage benefits and total compensation go back only to 1980. I label the two measures of pay based on those data as "compensation (ECI)" and "wages and salaries (ECI)."

A fourth source of wage data is the Current Population Survey (CPS), a survey of households used to collect the data for monthly reports on employment, unemployment, and the labor force. The unemployment rate is the best-known statistical product from that survey, but those data are used for numerous kinds of studies. One of the most important strengths of those data is that they permit analysis based on demographic and other variables. I refer to the wage measure based on those data as "average wages (CPS)."[23]

To make a realistic assessment of what has happened to the real pay that workers receive, I find it useful to see how some of those different measures of pay can be reconciled with each other. Compensation per hour (NA) is the most comprehensive, both for workers covered and for the components of pay included. By excluding nonwage benefits from total compensation, leaving a measure of wages and salaries per hour—wages and salaries (NA) (see figure 2–6)—we can see the importance of nonwage components of workers' pay.[24] The figure clearly shows that compensation per hour has increased more than measures of pay based on wages alone. Nonwage benefits increased more rapidly than wages, mainly before the 1980s. It is

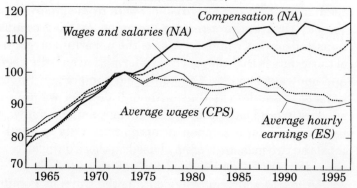

FIGURE 2–6

ALTERNATIVE MEASURES OF REAL WAGES AND COMPENSATION, 1963–1997

(Index: 1973 = 100)

NOTE: See the appendix for descriptions of the measurements. These four compensation measures are adjusted for inflation using CPI-U-X1.
SOURCE: Bureau of Labor Statistics; Bureau of the Census; and the Department of Commerce.

also clear, however, that nonwage benefits account for only a portion of the difference between compensation (NA) and average hourly earnings (ES). Finally, the cumulative increase in average wages based on data from the Current Population Survey does not differ very much from average hourly earnings (ES) despite the major differences in workers covered, wage concepts, and collection methods.[25]

For comparisons that include measures of pay based on Employment Cost Index data, it is necessary to focus on trends since 1980. Figure 2–7 shows measures of wages based on data from four different sources. Those data show a spectrum of wage trends that range between an approximately 5 percent increase or a decline in wages since 1980. The slump in average hourly earnings (ES) since 1980 is larger than for the other measures, as it has been since 1973.

Some of the differences in those wage measures may provide insights into differences in their trends. Wages and salaries (NA) are the most comprehensive of those

FIGURE 2–7
ALTERNATIVE MEASURES OF REAL WAGES, 1963–1997
(Index: 1980 = 100)

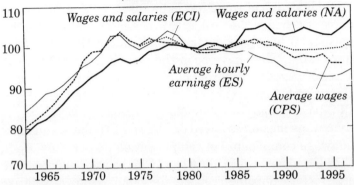

NOTE: See the appendix for descriptions of the measurements. These four compensation measures are adjusted for inflation using CPI-U-X1.

SOURCE: Bureau of Economic Analysis; Bureau of Labor Statistics; and Bureau of the Census.

measures for the kinds of wage payments they include. Wage payments made irregularly, such as bonuses or profit-sharing payments, are included in wages and salaries (NA) but not in wages and salaries (ECI). In the ECI-based data, such irregular wage payments are classified as benefits, and consequently those components of pay are included in compensation (ECI). That difference in treatment of irregular wage payments may be one reason why the ECI-based measure of wages and salaries increased less than the more comprehensive NA-based measure since 1975, when the ECI-based series began (see figure 2–7).

The CPS-based wage measure differs from the other series in several ways. It is, first of all, based on responses by family members to survey questions instead of on reports by business firms submitted for tax or other purposes. The CPS-based wage data reported here are for full-time adult workers and are calculated by excluding people whose estimated wages are in the top and bottom 10 percent of the distribution. The NA- and ECI-based measures include the wages and hours of part-time and part-year workers. In addition, the CPS-based wage data include government workers, in contrast to the other measures. The net effect of those and other differences is uncertain.[26]

Measures of wage levels based on CPS data are important because they constitute the main source of information on how particular components of the work force have fared. They have been the principal source of measures of wages for different demographic groups, for groups classified by age, years of schooling, race, and sex. Since CPS-based wage data show slower increases over the years than wage measures based on NA and ECI data, and since nonwage components of compensation do not show up in CPS-based wage data, data from CPS sources may be more satisfactory in some respects for comparisons of relative wages among different groups of workers than for measuring whether workers have been gaining or falling behind.

Figure 2–8 compares measures of both wages and compensation with average hourly earnings. The first point is that trends in real compensation since 1980 are reasonably similar according to the evidence from two entirely independent data sources. The increase in wages and salaries (NA) is closely comparable to the increase for compensation (NA). That is, according to those data, wages and salaries have increased at almost the same pace as benefits since 1980. Wages and salaries (ECI) hardly increased at all since 1980, compared with a 6 percent increase in wages and salaries (NA), probably in part because some components of wages and salaries included in the NA series are included as benefits instead in the ECI series. The second major point is that the ES-based measure of wages—average hourly earnings of production and nonsupervisory workers—shows a noticeable sag compared with the other measures of wages and the measures of compensation. That evidence is consistent with the earlier discussion emphasizing the limitations of the ES-based average hourly earnings data and their shortcomings as a measure of cumulative wage gains for the average worker.

It is useful to summarize at this point the shortcom-

FIGURE 2–8
ALTERNATIVE MEASURES OF REAL WAGES AND COMPENSATION,
1963–1997
(Index: 1980 = 100)

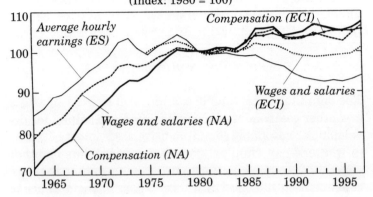

NOTE: See the appendix for descriptions of the measurements. All measures are adjusted for inflation using CPI-U-X1.
SOURCE: Bureau of Economic Analysis; Bureau of Labor Statistics; and Bureau of the Census.

ings of average hourly earnings of production and non-supervisory workers as a measure of how workers have fared. That measure covers a component of the work force with lower-than-average skills, and since the 1970s, wages of workers with relatively weaker skills increased less rapidly than skilled workers' wages. Average hourly earnings also cover only a portion of workers' pay. Nonwage benefits, which have increased more rapidly than wages over the years, are not included. In addition, irregular wage payments like bonuses and profit sharing are not included. Since the average hourly earnings measure is never benchmarked to reflect additional or more complete information, a cumulative measure of hourly earnings gains may fall behind gains that workers actually experience. Finally, regulatory and administrative rules that influence the sample have shifted the mixture of workers whose wages are included in the measure toward workers with lower wages. Consequently, average hourly earnings of production and nonsupervisory workers are seriously misleading as an indicator of how the average worker has fared because they systematically understate wage levels and pay gains.[27] On the basis of comparisons in figures 2–6 through 2–8, average hourly earnings apparently understate the trend of average wages by at least 15 percent since 1973 and by 5 to 10 percent since 1980.

Workers' Pay and Related Data

The data that are available from several sources on wages and other components of compensation are helpful for developing a reasonably comprehensive assessment of trends in workers' pay. Similarly, we can examine data on other aspects of economic performance to see whether they are consistent with trends in workers' pay. In the absence of other changes, for example, growth in real wages can be sustained only by corresponding increases in the value of output per hour of work. That is, we expect that, if appropriately measured, growth in compensation per hour of work should correspond closely to growth in labor productivity or output per hour of work. If workers were losing out, in the sense that increases in their pay were smaller than increases in their contribution to output, they would experience a decline in their share of the total value of the output of the economy. The proportion of total output paid in the form of labor compensation does vary over the business cycle, of course, but it has been fairly stable over the long term. Those observations lead to the expectation that growth in labor compensation should correspond fairly closely to growth in labor productivity.

Despite those expectations, comparison of productivity and pay trends as they have normally been measured since the early 1970s shows a considerable disparity. Productivity in the private sector has increased by almost a percentage point per year, on average, but compensation per hour has increased at about half that pace.[28] Why has workers' pay increased less rapidly? Two important factors that contribute to that disparity are differences in coverage of sectors of the economy and differences in measures of prices that are used to adjust for inflation.

Differences in coverage affect productivity and pay comparisons in a fairly straightforward way. Productivity measures that are usually cited are applicable to major sectors of the economy like the private business sector or the private nonfarm sector. The one percentage point per year figure cited above, for example, refers to the private nonfarm sector. One can compare those productivity figures with hourly compensation data for the same sector, of course, but such a comparison is incomplete. The government sector is treated by convention as if no productivity growth is realized there; the value of output in government is measured as the sum of the value of inputs. Government employment has in recent years accounted for about 16 percent of all employees on nonfarm payrolls. Increases in measured productivity that are realized in the private sector need to be shared with workers in the government sector, however; otherwise, wages of government employees would fall behind private-sector wages. Thus, wage gains for the economy as a whole are diluted by the fact that all workers need to share in the private-sector productivity gains, as we measure them.

The fact that analysts use different price indexes to measure real output and real wages is another reason for discrepancies between productivity and pay measures. What has happened to prices of computers—or more accurately, prices of computational capacity—provides an example of one type of difference in price measures. Computers are a more important item in an index of what workers produce than in an index of what families consume, because a large share of the computers produced are devoted to business equipment investment instead of to consumption. Consequently, because computer prices have declined sharply over the years, an index of output prices has increased substantially less rapidly than an index of consumer prices. That disparity has contributed to lower (measured) growth in real wages and compensation than measured growth in output per hour of work.

Other differences in price measurements also influence real output and consumption trends. For health services, for example, changes in what typical consumers need to pay out of their own pockets are used to measure prices for consumers, whereas the measure of prices used for real output in principle covers the value of all health services produced. Similarly, prices of some consumer items reflect the value of a flow of services that can be obtained from previously produced durable goods, and those services are not counted as part of current production. Prices of used cars are an example. Differences between price trends for the things that workers produce and the things that consumers buy lead to disparities between trends in measures of real productivity and pay.

Figure 2–9 illustrates the importance of differences in price measurements used to adjust for inflation. Real pay and productivity gains are much more closely comparable when the price measure used to compute the value of the output that workers produce is the same one used to adjust workers' pay for inflation.

In addition to those technical differences in price measurements that affect comparisons of productivity and pay, it is important to keep in mind the question of what we expect to accomplish by using a price index to adjust for inflation. A significant body of professional opinion—reflected, for example, in the report of the Boskin Commission—holds that the consumer price index has overstated price increases, perhaps by more than a percentage point per year.[29] That raises the question, of course, of just what is intended by adjustment for inflation. What exactly is the concept that the CPI overstates? The issues that arise in that context, from quality adjustment to treatment of new products to substitution possibilities, remind us that taking inflation into account by using the CPI is not necessarily the same as applying an adjustment for inflation that leaves consumers no better off than they were under a lower price pattern that prevailed earlier. That is, even if a measure of real pay shows no increase after adjustment for inflation, that result does not necessarily mean that the worker or consumer is no better off. At best, the

FIGURE 2–9
WORKERS' PRODUCTIVITY AND PAY IN THE NONFARM BUSINESS
SECTOR, 1959–1997
(Index: 1973 = 100)

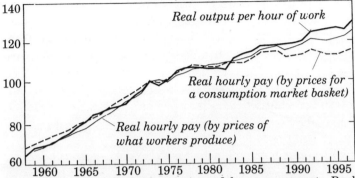

NOTE: See the appendix for descriptions of the measurements. Real
output per hour is adjusted for inflation using the implicit price
deflator for the nonfarm business economy; this price index is also
used to measure workers' pay in terms of prices of what they produce. To obtain real hourly pay in terms of its consumption value,
we deflated nominal wages using CPI-U-X1. Compensation per hour
is used as the basis for both measures of real hourly pay.
SOURCE: Bureau of Labor Statistics; U.S. Department of Labor; Bureau of Economic Analysis; and U.S. Department of Commerce.

CPI is not well designed to take into account changes in
the actual cost of living. Real levels of economic well-
being have accordingly almost surely improved by more
than conventional measures of real pay suggest.

We can more easily make a case for some adjustment
of real wages and compensation to offset an overstatement
of inflation by the CPI than justify a particular adjustment like the 1.1 percent per year estimated by the Boskin
Commission. Failure to make any adjustment at all is even
more difficult to justify, however. The Bureau of Labor
Statistics has already made several changes intended to
improve the index. During the past several years, for example, the BLS introduced changes in computational
methods to remove the effects of formula bias—changes
estimated on the basis of past experience to reduce the
rise in the price index by about 0.3 percent per year. We
can expect those changes and others that were introduced

FIGURE 2–10
ADJUSTED MEASURES OF REAL WAGES AND COMPENSATION,
1950–1997
(Index: 1973 = 100)

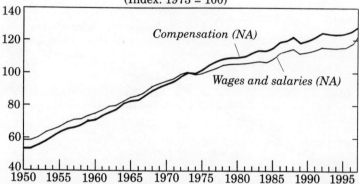

NOTE: See the appendix for descriptions of the measurements. In
addition to adjustment for inflation using CPI-U-X1, a further adjustment is made to the price index of one-half percentage point per
year beginning in 1978 to take into account changes in methodology
introduced by the BLS.
SOURCE: Bureau of Labor Statistics; Bureau of the Census; and Department of Commerce.

in January 1998 to reduce measured increases in the CPI
by at least half a percentage point per year.[30] Unless an
adjustment is made to reflect those changes, though, real
wages will appear to rise correspondingly more rapidly
after those changes have been phased in than they would
otherwise appear. If no adjustment is made, those changes
in BLS methods and procedures will result in an artificial
acceleration of real wage growth that is wholly attributable to changes in price measurement.

Some type of adjustment in the CPI as a measure of
price increases clearly seems to be appropriate to avoid a
distorted picture of price and real wage increases that occurred in the past. The purpose of the adjustment is to
produce an adjusted price measure that increases at the
same rate as it would have increased if current methods
and procedures had been used consistently over time. Such
an adjustment can be made by extending back over time
the estimated effects of the recent changes in CPI mea-

FIGURE 2–11
ADJUSTED MEASURES OF REAL WAGES AND COMPENSATION,
1963–1997
(Index: 1980 = 100)

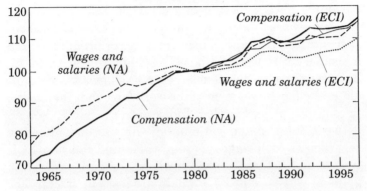

NOTE: See the appendix for descriptions of the measurements. In addition to an adjustment for inflation using CPI-U-X1, a further adjustment is made to the price index of one-half percentage point per year subsequent to 1978 to take into account changes in methodology introduced by the BLS.
SOURCE: Bureau of Economic Analysis; Bureau of Labor Statistics; and Bureau of the Census.

surement procedures—effects that were themselves estimated on the basis of historical data. Figures 2–10 and 2–11 chart adjusted real wage and compensation measures that reflect the estimated one-half percentage point per year smaller price increases. Extending the new methods back to 1978, when one of the most serious sources of overstatement was inadvertently introduced, increases real wage and compensation growth by almost 10 percent since 1980 and 12 percent since 1973. The cumulative differences that arise from even such seemingly small annual adjustments are noteworthy. The adjustment, for example, almost doubles estimated growth in real compensation since 1973 to close to 30 percent. Those estimates—which I regard as preferred estimates of how the average worker has fared economically—show an increase in real wages of at least 10 percent and an increase in compensation of about 15 percent since 1980.

Summary

The first conclusion I draw from the preceding discussion involves the measurement of wages. Each of the available measures of wages is subject to criticism, but the National Accounts–based measures emerge as superior in most respects. First, average hourly earnings of production and nonsupervisory workers, based on Employer Survey data, have very serious deficiencies, even as a measure of wages alone and for the segment of the work force that they cover. Second, Employment Cost Index data overstate the gap between total compensation and what is conventionally regarded as cash wages, so that wages and salaries (ECI) tend to understate the level of wages and may understate gains in wages. Third, CPS data are less satisfactory for measuring trends in real levels of workers' pay than for comparing trends in relative pay. Those comparisons suggest that we can regard National Accounts–based measures of compensation and wages and salaries as better measures of trends in the average level of workers' pay than those based on data from other sources. The trend those data show is also consistent with features of economic performance like productivity growth, in contrast to the wage measures that show the average worker falling behind.

The second and most important conclusion involves what those data mean for our understanding of the economy. In my view, they indicate that the conventional picture of a very substantial deterioration in the average level of real wages greatly exaggerates how poorly the average worker has fared. Instead of experiencing a substantial deterioration, workers have on average continued to realize small gains in their total compensation and, over the long term, even in the wages and salaries component of their pay. It is clear that most measures show that real pay has increased less rapidly since the early 1970s than during the 1950s and 1960s, and it is quite clear that slow growth in average real pay levels, combined with a decline in the relative pay of workers with the lowest skills, has meant that real wages have declined for some demographic groups. The average worker's total pay, however, has increased by about 15 percent since 1973, after adjustment for inflation using the conventional measure of consumer prices. If we apply the methodology now being used to measure price increases to adjust for inflation, we find that workers' average pay has increased by at least ten percentage points more, or more than 25 percent. That picture is significantly different from the portrayals of pervasive decline that have been commonplace in public discussions of how workers have fared.

3

The Distribution of Wages

The increase in wage dispersion that took place in the United States during the past twenty years is at least as noteworthy as the trend in the wage level. In the preceding chapter, I argued that, contrary to conventional wisdom, a realistic appraisal of the trend in the level of real wages indicates that the average worker's real pay has gone up instead of down. In my analysis of the distribution of wages, however, I do not take issue with the view that inequality has increased. Instead, I argue that analysts and commentators have frequently misunderstood the sources of the increase in wage inequality and that they have misinterpreted the consequences of greater skill-based wage dispersion.

The increase in U.S. wage inequality became apparent in the 1980s, but by some measures it began during the 1970s. A trend toward wider wage inequality was also noticeable in a number of other industrial countries. And although the United States experienced more widening of wage inequality than other countries, the United Kingdom also experienced a fairly pronounced change.[31] After two or three decades of little variation in the distribution of wages, the increase in inequality attracted a great deal of attention.

In the academic community, many research efforts and conferences have focused on describing and quantifying the increase in wage inequality, on identifying the fac-

FIGURE 3–1

RATIO OF WAGES AT THE EIGHTIETH PERCENTILE TO WAGES AT THE
TWENTIETH PERCENTILE OF THE DISTRIBUTION, 1961–1996

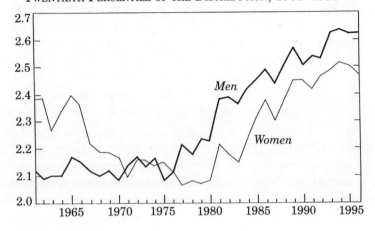

SOURCE: March CPS.

tors that contributed to increased inequality, and on looking for possible mitigating conditions.[32] Journalists and
commentators have expressed serious concerns about the
possible social and political consequences. Public policy
analysts have tried to diagnose the causes and effects and
develop proposals to counter them. The idea that wage
inequality was worsening and that it constituted a serious social problem came to be seen as a central theme in
discussions of many topics.[33]

Figure 3–1 shows simple measures of the increase in
wage inequality that took place over the past twenty years.
Those measures show the trend in the ratio of wages of
high-wage workers to those of workers with low wages.
High- and low-wage workers are identified simply on the
basis of their position in the wage distribution. Wages at
the twentieth and eightieth percentiles are the lower and
upper boundaries of the middle three quintiles of the distribution. Wages at the extremes do not affect that mea-

surement, and homogeneity of the workers is enhanced by considering only full-time workers who are twenty-five to fifty-four years old.[34] As those data show, the spread between wages at those points in the distribution has widened considerably and fairly steadily since the late 1970s. For males, the spread widened from a ratio of about 2.1 to more than 2.6.

The most common popular understanding of the changes taking place in the labor market emphasizes industrial change and the kinds of jobs that employers want to fill. When manufacturing jobs that paid good wages to high school–level workers disappeared, according to that line of reasoning, low-wage jobs in the service sector replaced those jobs. Wage dispersion accordingly increased, and the average level of wages was depressed.[35] From the point of view of business firms, skill requirements for new jobs were said to be quite low, and the wages firms needed to pay to fill the jobs were correspondingly low. According to that perspective, too many jobs that require too little skill exist, creation of low-wage jobs should be stifled, and creation of good jobs should be encouraged.

That approach to analyzing the problem is profoundly misleading. The effects of shifts in the employment mixture among industries, first of all, have been too small to account for the slowdown in growth in real wages and the increase in wage dispersion. Second, the inadequacy of that kind of explanation of wage stagnation is illustrated by examining employment shifts among occupations instead of among industries. In contrast to the pattern among industries, occupations that expanded more rapidly than average had higher average wages than those that expanded less rapidly or declined.[36] Clearly, shifts in the employment mixture among industries, occupations, and the like are not very helpful for explaining changes in wage patterns and trends.

Examining trends in relative wages in light of changes in the supply of and demand for labor with different levels of skill helps to structure an analysis of the main forces at work. On the supply side, although the proportion of the work force with high skills (measured by years of schooling and work experience) increased sharply throughout the 1970s and 1980s, the wages of high-skilled workers also rose relative to wages of the less skilled. Since wages of workers whose relative numbers were growing would normally be expected to decline in the absence of other changes, something else evidently changed.[37] Demand apparently shifted strongly in favor of workers with more skills, so that relative wages of skilled workers rose sharply despite the increase in their supply. Such a diagnosis of the source of the change in relative wages is exactly the opposite of the industry-mixture explanation that emphasizes creation of too many low-wage jobs. Relative wages for workers at the low end of the wage distribution apparently declined, not because workers could find only jobs that required little skill but because an excessive number of less-skilled workers were competing for such jobs, whose numbers were declining relative to jobs requiring higher skills.

If the basic cause of the shift in relative wages is a change in demand in favor of workers with better skills, what caused the change in demand? The main candidates are international trade and skill-biased technological change. The idea that trade might be an important factor seems plausible on two grounds: the straightforward observation that more trade often reduces opportunities for jobs at home for workers with low skills and the sophisticated theoretical reasoning about conditions for factor-price equalization.[38] But most professional economists have concluded that the empirical evidence provides little support for the view that international trade has been the major source of change in skill demands in the U.S. labor market.[39]

Skill-biased technical change has become the preferred explanation for an increase in the demand for labor skills. Although most of the evidence to support that view is indirect, evidence that higher pay is associated with computer use provides a bit of direct support.[40] And although many have viewed the growing use of computers as a likely source of demand for more highly skilled workers, we should not necessarily identify skill-biased technical change with high-technology production processes.

Analysts should evaluate the significance and the consequences of the increase in wage inequality from at least two different perspectives. The first involves workers' skills and the incentives to acquire them. The issues here include the extent to which increased wage inequality is associated with higher wages that firms pay for better skills, the awareness of workers about changes in skill premiums, and the strength of workers' responses to stronger incentives to improve their skills. Do stronger incentives for workers to invest in themselves lead to increases in schooling and skill development that will be beneficial to them and to the economy as a whole? The second perspective involves the extent to which the wider wage gaps between workers with different skill levels open up such large income differences that they are socially and politically divisive. That is, even if strengthening incentives for workers to invest in themselves is very important and if the improvement in skill levels contributes to higher living standards, are larger wage differences so disruptive of a sense of community and shared interests that it is, nevertheless, a bad idea to let the increased wage inequality emerge? I discuss both perspectives on the implications of the increase in wage inequality.

Skills and Incentives

Analysts can measure workers' skills only indirectly. Perhaps the best, and certainly the most widely used, general measure of workers' skills is years of schooling. Figure 3–2 shows the trend in the value of workers' skills on the

FIGURE 3–2
RATIO OF WAGES OF COLLEGE GRADUATES TO WAGES OF HIGH
SCHOOL GRADUATES, 1963–1996

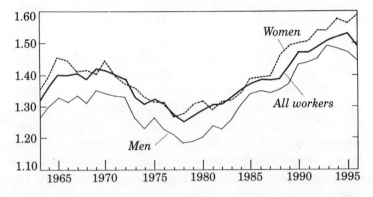

NOTE: Average wages were computed for the middle 80 percent of hourly wages for each group (the top and bottom 10 percent were excluded). Wages of workers with sixteen years of schooling are compared with those with twelve years of schooling.
SOURCE: March CPS.

basis of measures of wages for workers who completed high school and college. The first point that those data support is that the gap between average wages of high school and college graduates has widened considerably between the late 1970s and the mid-1990s. According to those data, men in their prime earning years who graduated from college earned almost 50 percent more than high school graduates in 1994 compared with only 20 percent more in the late 1970s. The increase for women was similar. The wage premium for skills, as measured by the college–high school wage ratio, increased very substantially during most of the past twenty years.

The second point is that the remarkable rise in the college wage premium that took place during the 1980s was in large part a recovery from a slump during the 1970s. The economic reward for attending and completing college declined to an unusually low level by the late 1970s, and we can regard part of the initial rise in the college premium as a return to a more normal level.[41] The college–high school wage premium has widened further since the late 1980s. The size of the increase in the schooling wage premium, however, is only about half as large when we measure it against a more normal base in the late 1960s as when we measure it against the late 1970s.

The pronounced decline in the college wage premium during most of the 1970s evidently resulted partly from the extraordinary bulge in numbers of young, college-educated workers who came into the work force when members of the baby-boom generation began to reach working age. The effect is shown most clearly among men. For young men just leaving college and entering the work force, the huge increase in numbers in the 1970s had the classic effect—a sharp decline in the wage premium for college attendance. College-educated men in their peak earnings years (ages forty-five to fifty-four) experienced essentially no decline during the 1970s in their wage premium relative to high school–level men in the same age category, and there was essentially no subsequent rise in the college wage premium for them (see figure 3–3).

The large number of college graduates just entering the work force in the 1970s led to a sharp increase in the proportion of the work force accounted for by people with college credentials. The increase was so large that by the mid-1970s young people between the ages of twenty and twenty-nine accounted for about a third of all college graduates of working age. Subsequently, the proportion of college graduates in their twenties gradually declined to the 25 percent range that prevailed in the mid-1960s. At the same time, differences in the college wage premium among men in different age categories were reduced to the point of approximate equality by the early 1990s.

Acquiring work experience and getting more years of schooling are alternative ways for workers to improve their

FIGURE 3–3

RATIO OF WAGES OF COLLEGE-EDUCATED MEN TO WAGES OF
HIGH SCHOOL–EDUCATED MEN, BY AGE CATEGORY,
1963–1996

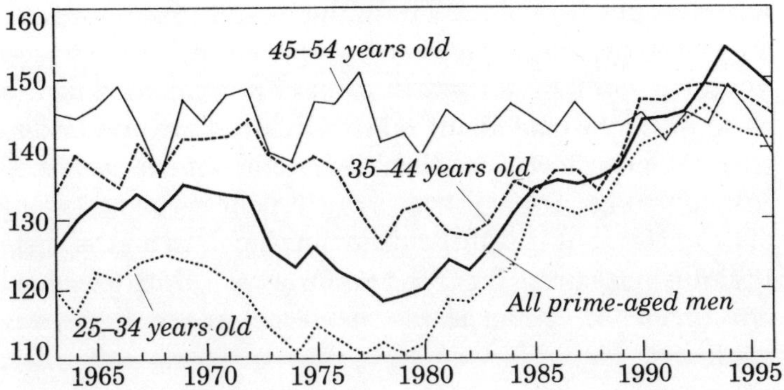

NOTE: See note to figure 3–2.
SOURCE: March CPS.

earning capability by investing in themselves.[42] The data
on wage trends for workers with different qualifications
in terms of years of schooling and work experience strongly
support the view that the increase in wage inequality that
took place during the past twenty years was in large part
attributable to increases in the economic rewards for skills.
That is, we cannot simply regard increased wage inequality as a capricious reshuffling of wages with the result that
"the rich get richer and the poor, poorer."[43] Wage inequality is instead a systematic result of major changes in the
value that the modern economy places on workers' skills.
The new wage relationships that emerged have important
effects on workers' incentives to invest in themselves by
developing their skills.

The relationship between the increase in wage inequality since the late 1970s and the increase in economic
rewards for the skills that workers bring to the labor market is the first important element in examining the contribution that economic incentives can make to developing a

highly skilled work force. Other important questions concern whether young people are sufficiently well informed about changes in economic rewards that have taken place and whether they are motivated to develop more skills in response to such changes in incentives. Do increased college wage premiums, for example, stimulate more young people to enroll in college? Business firms can be expected to be well informed about relative costs of hiring workers with different levels of schooling and about the costs and feasibility of training workers to compensate for schooling deficiencies, but it is difficult to develop data on the costs that business firms incur to train workers. Data on school enrollment of young people, however, are more readily available.

A good indicator of the extent to which young people respond to changes in the economic rewards for college is the proportion of people enrolled in postsecondary schools in the fall following their graduation from high school. Figure 3–4 shows college enrollment since 1963, along with a measure of the college–high school wage premium. The general shape of the pattern over time for both series is strikingly similar. Moreover, the increase in the enrollment rate since the late 1970s is quite large. Over a period of almost two decades, the proportion of high school graduates enrolled in postsecondary schooling rose from less than 50 percent to more than 60 percent. Youth who graduate from high school evidently become aware that better opportunities are open to them if they acquire additional schooling, and many are induced to extend their schooling to take advantage of those opportunities.

Inequality and Polarization

As has already been noted (in figures 3–2 and 3–4), the wage gap between workers with high school and college credentials widened enormously from the late 1970s to the mid-1990s. The average wage of a mature adult college

FIGURE 3–4
College Enrollment and College Wage Premium, 1963–1996

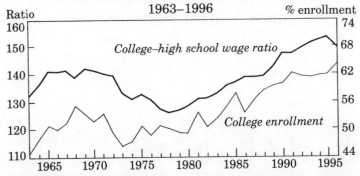

NOTE: Enrollment figures are the percentage of high school graduates aged sixteen to twenty-four who were enrolled in college in the October following graduation. Average wages were computed for the middle 80 percent of hourly wages for full-time workers aged twenty-five to fifty-four (the top and bottom 10 percent were excluded). Wages of workers with sixteen years of schooling are compared with those with twelve years of schooling.
SOURCE: Bureau of the Census and March CPS.

graduate was about 25 percent higher in 1978 than the wage of a high school graduate. By 1995, the difference had more than doubled to an average wage that was more than 50 percent higher for the college-educated worker. Some observers have described the difference between high school and college-level workers as a great divide, with only college graduates able to earn a reasonably adequate living while their high school–level counterparts increasingly fell behind.[44] To what extent is that a realistic characterization of workers and their wages?

It is certainly true that on average wages of college-educated workers are significantly higher than for high school–level workers and that the gap between those averages has increased. As a consequence, the payoff for going to college, on average, has increased. But focusing only on averages masks a great deal of diversity. Wages that are actually paid to workers in both those schooling cat-

FIGURE 3–5
WAGE DISTRIBUTIONS AND MEDIAN WAGE FOR HIGH SCHOOL AND
COLLEGE GRADUATES, 1996
(percentage of educational category)

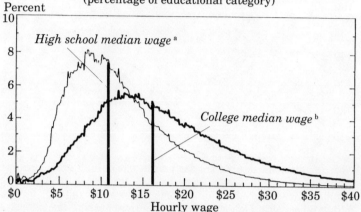

NOTE: Histograms calculated on $0.10 increments in wage levels.
Histograms have been smoothed using a symmetric moving average filter with a width equal to ± 20 percent of the wage level.
a. Median high school wage, $11.00 per hour.
b. Median college wage, $16.34 per hour.
SOURCE: March 1997 CPS.

egories are distributed across a fairly wide range, as illustrated in figure 3–5. The figure also shows hourly earnings at the high school median of $11 per hour and hourly earnings about 50 percent higher for college-level workers. The distributions charted there show, for example, that many high school–level workers earn more than the median for college-level workers and that many college-level workers earn less than the median for workers with only high school credentials. Some of the overlap in those wage distributions reflects differences in skills and earning capabilities for workers with the same years of schooling, and some of the overlap reflects choices workers make about jobs, wages, and other conditions of work. The general point is that the two distributions overlap a great deal. Averages or medians tell a useful story, but not the whole story.

FIGURE 3–6
PERCENTAGE OF HIGH SCHOOL GRADUATES EARNING LESS THAN
THE MEDIAN WAGE FOR COLLEGE GRADUATES, 1963–1996

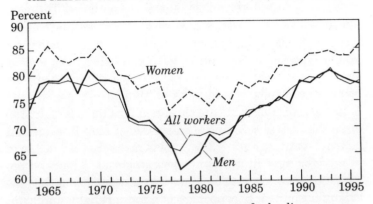

NOTE: Wages of workers with sixteen years of schooling are compared with those with twelve years of schooling.
SOURCE: March CPS.

The amount of overlap between the high school and college wage distributions was, of course, reduced when the difference between their means widened. As figure 3–6 shows, the proportion of high school graduates who earned less than the college median declined when the average college wage premium declined and increased subsequently when the college wage premium rose. By the mid-1990s, about 20 percent of high school–educated men earned more than the median for their college-level counterparts. That proportion was a decline from about 35 percent in the late 1970s. Fifty percent is, of course, the relevant reference point for distributions that are identical. Consequently, I view those data as showing a great deal of overlap in the wages of college and high school graduates, even in recent years when the amount of overlap was reduced as the difference in average wages between workers with different education levels widened.

To see whether high school– and college-level workers may have less in common than those comparisons of their earnings distributions suggest, we need to consider the sensitivity of those comparisons to workers' age and work experience. That is, on average, earnings rise as workers accumulate additional work experience. The overlap in earnings distributions of high school and college graduates accordingly could mainly reflect a tendency for many high school graduates with extensive work experience to earn wages comparable to those of young and inexperienced college graduates. In that case, those in similar stages of their working careers might have less in common than suggested by data that do not take into account age differences. Figure 3–7 reports measures of overlap in wages for men in different age categories. The relationship between age and earnings is more apparent for men than for women, because age is a more reliable indicator of work experience for men. Those data show changes in the extent of overlap in wage distributions for college- and high school–level men that are much more pronounced for younger workers. That pattern is closely comparable to the one for changes in the ratios of average wages shown in figure 3–3. For both measures, the pronounced differences between age categories that opened up in the 1970s fell sharply by the early 1990s.

The amount of overlap between distributions of wages of high school and college graduates is apparently not attributable mainly to differences in the age or career status of workers. Although the average wages of most college-educated workers are considerably higher than those of high school graduates, the wage levels of both groups have a great deal in common. It should be noted that by this measure—the position in the high school distribution of the college median—the separation between wages of workers in those two schooling categories is no wider in the early 1990s than it was in the late 1960s. Perhaps current distributional patterns are accordingly not substantially more divisive than patterns that prevailed thirty years ago.

High school and college graduates are significant com-

FIGURE 3–7
PERCENTAGE OF HIGH SCHOOL GRADUATES EARNING LESS
THAN THE MEDIAN WAGE FOR COLLEGE GRADUATES, FOR MEN
BY AGE CATEGORY, 1963–1996

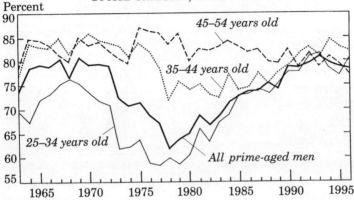

NOTE: See figure 3–6.
SOURCE: March CPS.

ponents of the adult work force, with high school graduates accounting for about 30 percent and college graduates for about 20 percent of the total. The next most important group is intermediate between those two categories—people who graduated from high school and have
some postsecondary schooling but less than four years or
a college degree. They account for almost another 30 percent of the adult work force. Their average wage is intermediate between wages of college- and high school–level
workers, and overlaps in the distribution of their wages
with both high school and college graduates are large.
Taken together, those groups with much overlapping in
their wage distributions account for about 80 percent of
the adult work force. The remaining two groups—high
school dropouts (with the lowest wages) and postgraduate
professionals (with the highest wages)—each account for
roughly 10 percent of workers. Table 3–1 reports median
wage levels and proportions of the adult work force ac-

TABLE 3-1

MEDIAN WAGE AND PERCENTAGE OF THE WORK FORCE
BY EDUCATIONAL CATEGORY, 1996

Educational Category	Median Wage (dollars)	Percentage of Work Force
High school dropout	7.77	10
High school graduate	11.00	32
Some college	12.66	28
College graduate	16.24	20
Postgraduate	21.15	10

SOURCE: March 1997 CPS.

counted for by workers in each educational category. Those data help to underscore the point that workers in the United States are not sharply divided along lines that are marked by differences in schooling and wage levels.

An alternative to showing differences in median wages in relation to major schooling categories like high school and college graduates (figure 3–8) is to show fractions of workers in the various schooling classes who earn more or less than the median wage for adult workers. In figure 3–9 I show cumulative distributions of wages of workers in all five broad schooling categories. Those data show, for example, that about half the workers with some college earn more than the median wage for adult workers as a whole, as might be expected for workers in a schooling category close to the middle. More than four of five workers with graduate or professional degrees earn more than the median for the total, however, compared with about one of five for high school dropouts. Looking at the data arranged in that way underscores the point that a great deal of overlap exists in wage distributions for workers in the schooling categories that encompass most workers and that, although the extent of the overlap decreases, it does not entirely disappear even when we consider work-

FIGURE 3–8
WAGE DISTRIBUTION OF HIGH SCHOOL AND COLLEGE GRADUATES
AND MEDIAN WAGES BY EDUCATIONAL CATEGORY, 1996
(percentage of educational category)

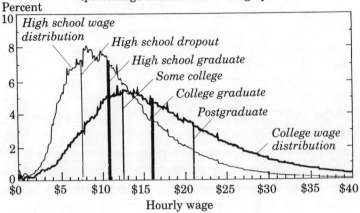

NOTE: See figure 3–5.
SOURCE: March 1997 CPS.

FIGURE 3–9
CUMULATIVE EARNINGS DISTRIBUTIONS BY EDUCATION FOR FULL-
TIME WORKERS AGED TWENTY-FIVE TO FIFTY-FOUR, 1996

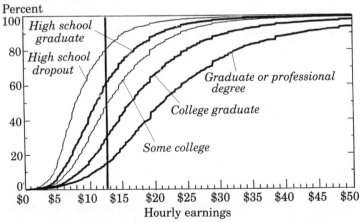

NOTE: Median wage is $12.66 per hour.
SOURCE: March 1997 CPS.

ers in the highest and lowest schooling categories.

With regard to a group like high school dropouts, it is important to recognize that sometimes ostensibly comparable demographic groups differ in ways that have quite important effects on earning capabilities. Those differences affect both wage levels and relative wage comparisons. Comparisons are sometimes made, for example, between wages of high school dropouts and others, or changes in wage levels for dropouts are traced over time. The problem is that although age and years of schooling may be similar for the workers compared, other characteristics may be very different. Failure to attend or complete high school, for example, was much more common a generation ago than now. Dropout status now increasingly raises questions about personal discipline and commitment. Questions also arise about whether people are different in ways that may be even more important for successful job performance than years of school completed. Having a criminal record has a devastating effect on earnings capability, for instance, and young high school dropouts are disproportionately affected. Consequently, the decline that has occurred in the real wage level of young dropouts overstates the decline attributable to dropout status by itself.[45]

It is important to recognize that although differences in average earnings are quite large between workers in different schooling categories, like high school and college graduates, dispersion of wages within each group is also quite large. Even though average earnings of college graduates are about 50 percent higher than for high school graduates, for example, about 20 percent of high school graduates still earn wages that are higher than the median earnings of college graduates.[46] That is an important reminder that years of schooling indicate an individual's earning capability only crudely. Education and work experience together are very useful, but also very incomplete, measures of workers' skills and the value of those skills in the marketplace.

4

Conclusions

Two views about the labor market have become so common that they can be reasonably regarded as the conventional wisdom. The first is that the average worker's real pay has been stagnant for many years. The second is that wage inequality has increased significantly, so that the gap between the poor and the better off has widened. The idea that either of those developments would be more tolerable if the other had not occurred provides an important link between those two views. Thus, for example, it is more difficult to defend the legitimacy of a shift in relative pay in favor of workers with managerial and professional skills if that is accompanied by an actual decline in the real wages of many of the workers most directly involved in producing goods and services. The fairness of a process in which some are perceived as gaining at the expense of others is easier to question than one in which all workers are seen as gaining, even though some gain more than others. Not surprisingly, conventional wisdom about the labor market frequently serves as a point of reference for expressions of concern about the economic, social, and political implications and as the premise for advocacy of policies intended to reverse, or at least moderate, recent trends.

In the first part of this volume, I argue that analysts and commentators have exaggerated the extent to which workers' pay has stagnated or declined. The main reason is that they have placed excessive credence on a widely cited measure of wages that understates the average worker's pay level and the real gains the average worker has realized. Average hourly earnings of production and nonsupervisory workers are so flawed and incomplete a measure that we should not regard them as a realistic measure of trends in the average worker's wages; and we should not use average hourly earnings to set even a plausible lower boundary for a range of estimates of average wages. In addition, we need to take into account nonwage benefits and problems with the index of prices used to calculate real wages to appraise realistically how the average worker has fared. In my view, the data support the conclusion that the real wage of the average worker has increased by about 15 percent during the past twenty-five years instead of declining and that the average worker's total pay has increased more than 25 percent. Those numbers represent a slowdown in real wage growth since the 1950s and 1960s but not complete stagnation or pervasive deterioration.

In the second part of this volume, I argue that although an increase in wage inequality has occurred during the past twenty years, analysts and commentators have not well understood its sources and consequences. First, the increase in wage inequality mainly reflects increased economic rewards for schooling and skills. Second, we should view much of the increase in wage premiums for schooling that took place since the late 1970s as a recovery from unusually low wage premiums then. Third, the greater economic rewards to schooling have brought about a strong increase in the proportion of young people enrolled in postsecondary schooling. Fourth, despite a pronounced increase in the gap between the average wages of high school and college graduates, wages of workers in both groups are widely dispersed. Consequently, analysts and commentators have exaggerated the degree of polar-

ization or separation of workers in those important schooling categories and have overemphasized the likely adverse
social and political consequences of the increase in skill
premiums.

Definitions of Measures Reported in Figures

Average hourly earnings: These data refer to production and nonsupervisory workers in the private nonfarm sector. The data are generated by monthly surveys of employers under the Current Employment Statistics (CES) program, and they are sometimes referenced as the 790 series. This wage series is labeled "average hourly earnings (ES)" to reflect its source from an Employers' Survey, when it is necessary to distinguish between these data and related wage measures from other sources.

Average wages (CPS): Wages are based on data from the Current Population Survey. The average is calculated as a trimmed mean, with workers with highest 10 percent of wages and lowest 10 percent excluded. The data cover full-time workers aged twenty-five to fifty-four in the earner study sample of the Current Population Survey. Workers were selected for inclusion based on the following characteristics: (1) the longest job in the reporting year was not farm, self-employed and unincorporated, or without pay; (2) workers were employed full-time in the reporting year; and (3) workers reported working more than thirteen weeks in the reporting year. Hourly earnings for individual workers were calculated from the CPS data by dividing their wage and salary income by total weeks worked in the reporting year to obtain average weekly earnings, and then dividing average weekly earnings by hours worked per week in the reporting year.

Average weekly earnings: These data (reported in figure 2–1) are for production and nonsupervisory workers. The data are collected in the same monthly surveys of employers that are used to generate average hourly earnings measures for those same workers. When they are adjusted for inflation by using the same price index, the difference in the trend in average weekly earnings from that for average hourly earnings reflects only the trend of average weekly hours of work reported for those workers.

Compensation per hour: These data include wages and salaries of employees, plus employers' contributions for social insurance and private benefit plans. The principal source for these data is the ES-202 program, a cooperative effort between the Bureau of Labor Statistics and the states for reports on workers covered by unemployment insurance laws. This series is labeled "compensation per hour (NA)" to reflect its origins in data developed for the National Income and Product Accounts when it is necessary to distinguish between this data series and related data from other sources.

Compensation (ECI): This is a measure of compensation—wages and benefits—based on data collected from employers under the Employment Cost Index program of the Bureau of Labor Statistics. This program was begun during the 1970s to collect comprehensive data on wage and nonwage costs of employment. The data reported in the figures cover private nonfarm workers.

Median family income: These data (reported in figure 2–1) are official statistics reported regularly by the Bureau of the Census. The underlying information for these data is collected by annual supplements to the Current Population Survey.

Median hourly earnings and median wages: These are medians for particular groups of workers calculated from the same underlying data as average wages (CPS) for the same sample from the Current Population Survey that is used for the other CPS-based measures.

Regulatory test wage: This is the wage level (reported in figure 2–5) that serves as one of the criteria for administrative classification of workers as exempt from the minimum wage and overtime provisions of the Fair Labor Standards Act. The other main criteria under the administrative regulations used to determine exempt status of workers involve duties and responsibilities of workers. (See text and notes 15 through 19 for additional details.)

Wages and salaries (ECI): This is a measure of wages based on data collected under the Employment Cost Index program. (See also the entry for compensation (ECI) for a discussion of data from this source.)

Wages and salaries (NA): This is a measure of average wages per hour based on National Income and Product Accounts data. This measure was calculated by multiplying compensation per hour by the ratio of total wages and salaries to total compensation for each year in the data series to remove the effects of nonwage benefits on the index of compensation per hour. (See also the entry for compensation per hour for a discussion of data from this source.)

Notes

1. The quotation is from an op-ed article by Laura D'Andrea Tyson, "Inequality amid Prosperity," *Washington Post*, July 9, 1997.

2. Both average weekly earnings and median family income in figure 2–1 are adjusted for inflation by using the consumer price index (CPI). Compensation per hour in figure 2–2 is adjusted for inflation by using CPI-U-X1, an index with housing costs measured in a way that is consistent over time by substituting a rental-equivalence measure of owner-occupied housing from 1967 to 1983. During those years the average increase in the CPI was about half a percentage point higher per year than for CPI-U-X1 (*Economic Report of the President*, February 1997, table B.60, p. 368).

3. Lawrence Mishel and Jared Bernstein, *The State of Working America: 1994–95* (Washington, D.C.: Economic Policy Institute, 1994); Robert B. Reich, *The Work of Nations: Preparing Ourselves for the 21st Century* (New York: Alfred A. Knopf, Inc., 1991); John B. Judis, "Why Your Wages Keep Falling," *New Republic,* February 14, 1994, pp. 26–39; Jack Beatty, "Who Speaks for the Middle Class?" *Atlantic Monthly*, May 1994; and John Cassidy, "Who Killed the Middle Class?" *New Yorker,* October 16, 1995, pp.113–24, are examples.

4. Tyson, "Inequality amid Prosperity."

5. Lester Thurow, *The Future of Capitalism* (New York: William Morrow and Company, 1996), p. 2.

6. Transcript of *NewsHour* panel, Academics on Economic Insecurity, March 19, 1996.

7. *Breaking the Social Contract: The Fiscal Crisis in Higher Education,* Report of the Commission on National Investment in Higher Education, Council for Aid to Education, an Independent Subsidiary of RAND, 1997, p. 5.

8. It is important to note that both series charted in figure 2–3 (and in most subsequent figures) are adjusted for inflation by using CPI-U-X1, like compensation per hour in figure 2–2 but in contrast

to the series in figure 2–1. Also note that the trend for average hourly earnings (charted in figure 2–3) differs from the more pronounced downward trend in average weekly earnings (charted in figure 2–1) because of both the difference in price indexes and the decline in average weekly hours of work for workers covered by those data.

9. The publications cited as examples in note 3, and most references in newspaper articles and periodicals, rely extensively on average hourly earnings of production and nonsupervisory workers to support arguments that the typical worker has fallen behind in recent years.

10. Chapter 3 of this volume discusses the decline in the relative wages of workers with lower skill levels. A discussion of workers who are reported as production and nonsupervisory workers appears in the next section.

11. Some components of total compensation are not seen by workers on their pay statements, such as employers' contributions for Social Security. Other components are seen on their pay statements but not realized in their take-home pay, such as the payroll taxes withheld from workers for Social Security and for Medicare.

12. There seems to be little trend in the proportion of private industry workers covered by major collective bargaining agreements with lump-sum payment provisions. It has varied some from year to year but was 42 percent in 1987 and 45 percent in 1995. See *Monthly Labor Review,* January 1993, pp. 8–9, and other more recent issues.

13. In news releases in late January 1998, the three major domestic automobile companies reported the following profit-sharing bonus payments: Chrysler, $4,600; Ford, $4,480; and General Motors, $750. *Automotive News,* March 9, 1998, reported that workers at Saturn might receive bonuses of $5,000 compared with only $2,000 in the previous year. Chrysler employees were reported to have received bonuses of $8,000 last year in *Automotive News*, March 3, 1997. In the previous year, hourly workers in the automobile industry were reported to have received annual average profit-sharing payments as follows: Chrysler, $3,200; Ford, $1,700; General Motors (except Saturn), $800; and Saturn, $10,000 (*Wall Street Journal,* February 1, 1996). Although commentary on pay, performance, and incentives often suggests that irregular wage payments are becoming more common (see, for example, Steven Pearlstein, "The Quiet Revolution: Linking Pay to the Bottom Line," *Washington Post,* November 21, 1996), systematic information on trends of its prevalence is difficult to obtain.

14. Employment totals are benchmarked annually, and adjustments are sometimes quite sizable.

15. The regulations are described, for example, in *The Fair Labor Standards Act of 1938, as Amended,* U.S. Department of Labor, Employment Standards Administration, Wage and Hour Division, WH Publication 1318, revised August 1991.

16. In a very useful paper, "Divergent Trends in Alternative Real Wage Series," Katherine G. Abraham, James R. Spletzer, and Jay C. Stewart (Bureau of Labor Statistics, August 14, 1997) present evidence that outside of goods-producing industries, wage trends for nonexempt workers correspond quite closely to trends reported for production and nonsupervisory workers.

17. Title 29, Part 541, of the Code of Federal Regulations contains a set of effective date notes at relevant sections indicating that revisions were made on January 13, 1981, but "in accordance with the President's memorandum of January 29, 1981 (46 FR 11227, Feb. 6, 1981), the effective date was postponed indefinitely at 46 FR 11972, Feb. 12, 1981."

18. Actually, the regulations specify two sets of wage and duties tests, with some differentiation by occupational categories. To qualify as exempt, workers can meet either a more stringent set of conditions with respect to duties and a lower (long-test) wage or less stringent duties requirements and a higher (short-test) wage. The long-test wage levels (adjusted for inflation) that are charted in figure 2–4 are based on wage and salary levels for executive and administrative personnel (converted to estimated hourly wages based on a forty-hour week). The short-test wage follows a similar pattern over time at a higher wage level. Workers need to meet a longer list of duties specifications to qualify as exempt at the long-test wage, while at the higher short-test wage they can qualify under a shorter list of duties specifications. Long- and short-test wage levels for executive and administrative personnel are $155 per week and $250 per week, respectively. The duties tests involve at least some management responsibilities and direction of the work of at least two employees. To qualify for exemption, most professionals are subject to a somewhat higher long-test wage, computer professionals are subject to a separate set of rules, and sales workers are largely exempt, as well as employees in some seasonal and recreational jobs (among others). A peek into the complexity of regulations governing exemptions from some provisions is available from the *Handy Reference Guide to the Fair Labor Standards Act,* U.S. Department of Labor, Employment Standards Administration, Wage and Hour Division, WH Publication 1282, revised October 1994.

19. Practitioners widely agree that the wage tests are now irrelevant for determining exempt status. But that was apparently not the case in the late 1970s, and it would presumably not be the case now if wage test levels had been raised periodically in the 1980s and 1990s as they had been previously. The tests for exempt status are so problematic and anomalous in their application that some analysts have suggested that the duties tests should be abandoned in favor of a less ambiguous (and higher) wage test alone.

20. Those data are generated by monthly surveys of employers under the Current Employment Statistics (CES) program, and those data are also sometimes referenced as the 790 series.

21. Practitioners usually refer to those data on the basis of their National Income and Product Accounts (NIPA) origins. The principal source for those data is the ES-202 program, a cooperative effort between the Bureau of Labor Statistics and the states under which they report on workers covered by the unemployment insurance laws.

22. The Employment Cost Index program was begun during the 1970s to gather comprehensive information on wage and nonwage costs of employment.

23. The wage data that I report from the CPS are based on the March survey that covers work and earnings during the preceding year. The wage series I report are for prime-age (twenty-five to fifty-four years old), full-time workers. Hourly wages are estimated as annual earnings divided by the product of weeks of work and estimated weekly hours of work. Weekly hours are estimated for 1975 and the years following by relating usual hours of work to age, race, schooling, weeks worked, and usual hours worked. Weekly working hours are estimated, and weeks within reported intervals are imputed by using that estimating relationship for years before 1975. In addition, averages are computed as trimmed means, excluding the top and bottom 10 percent. This procedure sidesteps the problem of what to do with top-coded observations, and it also reduces the extent to which averages are heavily influenced by workers at the low end of the wage distribution. For comparison with other series, note that the other wage series are essentially hours-weighted instead of people-weighted. The data were extracted from March CPS Utilities CD files developed by Unicon Research Corporation, Santa Monica, California.

24. The wages and salaries (NA) figures are calculated by multiplying compensation per hour by the ratio of total compensation minus supplements to wages and salaries to total compensation for each year in the data series. The results of those calculations closely approximate the wages and salaries counterpart to total compensation per hour.

25. The coverage of data on average wages from the Current Population Survey was not chosen to replicate other wage series or to be closely comparable to the coverage of data from other wage series. The CPS wage data were instead constructed to represent wages of adult, full-time workers in the economy. For careful comparisons of CPS wage measures for similar workers, see Abraham, Spletzer, and Stewart, "Divergent Trends." Wage measures from the CPS may also be affected by the influence of self-reporting on differences between total and take-home pay and by differences in hours trends.

26. Wages from sources other than the CPS generally include employees of private business firms, with allowance for the self-employed in the case of the NA-based estimates.

27. After reviewing several measures of real wages, Barry

Bosworth and George Perry conclude that "real wages have stagnated over the past two decades, but claims of a large decline in the average real wage are exaggerated." "Among measures of wages and compensation," they write, "the hourly earnings index should be dismissed." "Productivity and Real Wages: Is There a Puzzle?" *Brookings Papers on Economic Activity,* no. 1, 1994, p. 328.

In "Divergent Trends," Abraham, Spletzer, and Stewart also conclude that the average hourly earnings of production and nonsupervisory workers series is an outlier after careful, detailed comparisons with other wage measures.

28. Productivity—output per hour of work—in the business sector increased by about a percentage point per year from 1973 to 1996, and it increased slightly less in the nonfarm business sector. Real compensation per hour increased by about half a percentage point per year when adjusted for inflation using CPI-U-X1, but only about a third of a percentage point using the CPI.

29. Michael J. Boskin, *Toward a More Accurate Measure of the Cost of Living,* Final Report to the Senate Finance Committee, from the Advisory Commission to Study the Consumer Price Index, December 4, 1996. For a very useful and informative discussion of the issues raised by the report and reactions of professionals in government and at universities, see the series of six articles published in the *Journal of Economic Perspectives,* vol. 12, no. 1 (Winter 1998), pp. 3–78.

30. That is a conservative estimate based in part on estimates developed by the Bureau of Labor Statistics and the Congressional Budget Office and reported in a mimeo, "The Consumer Price Index: Current Methods and Procedures, and Methodological Issues and Improvements," U.S. Bureau of Labor Statistics, October 13, 1997. See also the discussion of methodological changes in the *Economic Report of the President,* February 1998, pp. 79–80. When additional changes in CPI methodology that are currently scheduled for 1999 are introduced, still further adjustment of earlier data will be necessary to avoid distortion of price, output, and wage trends.

31. See, for example, Organization for Economic Cooperation and Development, "Employment/Unemployment Study Interim Report by the Secretary General," OECD/GD (93)102 (Paris: OECD, 1993). See also OECD, *The OECD Jobs Study: Unemployment in the OECD Area, 1950–1995* (Paris: OECD, 1994); OECD, *Evidence and Explanations, Part I, Labor Market Trends and Underlying Forces of Change* (Paris: OECD, 1994); and OECD, *Evidence and Explanations, Part II, The Adjustment Potential of the Labor Market* (Paris: OECD, 1994, table 7.A.1, pp. 160–61).

32. Frank Levy and Richard J. Murnane review much of the early research on those issues in "U.S. Earnings Levels and Earnings Inequality: A Review of Recent Trends and Proposed Explanations," *Journal of Economic Literature* (September 1992). The National

Bureau of Economic Research carried out a major project of research, working papers, conferences, and publications to document and analyze changes in the structure of wages in the United States and other countries. See also Jagdish Bhagwati and Marvin H. Kosters, *Trade and Wages: Leveling Wages Down?* (Washington, D.C.: AEI Press, 1994); and Adrian Wood, *North-South Trade, Employment, and Inequality: Changing Fortunes in a Skill-Driven World* (New York: Oxford University Press and Clarendon Press, 1994). See Gary Burtless, "International Trade and the Rise in Earnings Inequality," *Journal of Economic Literature,* vol. 32 (June 1995), pp. 800–816, for a review of contemporary analyses. For a comprehensive recent review and analysis, see William Cline, *Trade and Income Distribution* (Washington, D.C.: Institute for International Economics, 1997).

33. Examples include Kevin Phillips, *The Politics of Rich and Poor: Wealth and the American Electorate in the Reagan Aftermath* (New York: Random House, 1990); James A. Auerbach and Richard S. Belous, eds., *The Inequality Paradox: Growth of Income Disparity* (Washington, D.C.: National Policy Association, 1998); and Aspen Institute, *Work and Future Society: Where Are the Economy and Technology Taking Us?* (Washington, D.C.: Aspen Institute, 1998).

34. See note 23 for a description of the CPS sample.

35. That reasoning, along with examples used to illustrate it, can be found in articles in numerous newspapers and periodicals. An article in the August 28, 1997, *Wall Street Journal*, "The Changing Lot of the Hourly Worker," fits the pattern. In a brief introductory section, the article noted that Wal-Mart had just passed General Motors as the nation's largest employer. The paper then ran two separate articles that related the experience of a man working at General Motors in Kansas City, Kansas, and a woman working at Wal-Mart in suburban St. Louis, Missouri, to employment and wage developments in the country as a whole. As the introduction helpfully explained, "The shift is more than symbolic. Union jobs with lush pay and benefits, like the one held by GM assembly-line worker Tim Philbrick, are disappearing. In their place are nonunion jobs like that of Nancy Handley, who works in the men's department at a Missouri Wal-Mart."

36. For a comparison of industry job trends and wage levels, see Joseph R. Meisenheimer II, "The Service Industry in the 'Good' vs. 'Bad' Jobs Debate," *Monthly Labor Review*, vol. 121, no. 2 (February 1998), pp. 24–47. For a discussion of occupational job growth, see *Economic Report of the President*, February 1997, pp. 142–43.

37. The increase in the relative wages of skilled workers at the time when the schooling and work experience of the work force were being upgraded is demonstrated by Kevin M. Murphy and Finis Welch, "The Role of International Trade in Wage Differentials," in *Workers and Their Wages: Changing Patterns in the United States,*

Marvin H. Kosters, ed. (Washington, D.C.: AEI Press, 1991).

38. See, for example, Jagdish Bhagwati and Vivek H. Dehejia, "Freer Trade and Wages of the Unskilled—Is Marx Striking Again?" pp. 36–75, and Alan V. Deardorff and Dalia S. Hakura, "Trade and Wages—What Are the Questions?" pp. 76–107, in Bhagwati and Kosters, *Trade and Wages.*

39. See, for example, Cline, *Trade and Income Distribution,* and Paul R. Krugman and Robert Z. Lawrence, "Trade, Jobs, and Wages," *Scientific American,* vol. 270, no. 4 (April 1994). For a good introduction to differences in viewpoints on that issue, see Richard B. Freeman, "Are Your Wages Set in Beijing?"; J. David Richardson, "Income Inequality and Trade: How to Think, What to Conclude,"; and Adrian Wood, "How Trade Hurt Unskilled Workers," all in *Journal of Economic Perspectives,* vol. 9, no. 3 (Summer 1995).

40. The evidence that is usually cited is Alan B. Krueger, "How Computers Have Changed the Wage Structure: Evidence from Microdata, 1984–1989," *Quarterly Journal of Economics,* vol. 108 (February 1993), pp. 33–60. See also David Autor, Lawrence Katz, and Alan Krueger, "Computing Inequality: Have Computers Changed the Labor Market?" NBER Working Paper no. 5956, for a review of other evidence on the effects of technology on the structure of wages.

41. A very useful framework for examining wage relationships to determine whether earnings forgone while obtaining additional schooling compare favorably with the economic rewards is presented in Sherwin Rosen, "The Market for Lawyers," *Journal of Law and Economics* (October 1992), pp. 215–46.

42. The wage premium for work experience was higher in the 1980s than in the late 1960s and early 1970s for both high school and college graduates, but the timing and size of the increases were different. The work experience wage premium increased more rapidly for college than for high school graduates in the 1970s when the influx of young college graduates was most pronounced. But the work experience premium for high school graduates rose further in the 1980s when it stabilized for college graduates.

43. The underlying reason why inequality increases is probably more often described by journalists in terms of greed than of chance. The well-off are often described as gaining at the expense of the poor. A news article by Christina Duff describing newly released data on income trends in 1996, for example, asked why the poverty rate did not improve. (The poverty rate actually did show a one-tenth percentage point decrease to 13.7 percent, but that change was not statistically significant.) Her answer: "Because the wealthiest Americans grabbed most of the income gains. Average income for the poorest 20 percent of the population slid 1.8 percent in 1996, while average earnings for the wealthiest 20 percent climbed 2.2 percent." She returned to that theme a paragraph later when she described earlier years as worse, "when the rich grabbed increas-

ingly larger shares at the expense of the poor and middle class" ("Household Income Rose Again in 1996," *Wall Street Journal,* September 30, 1997). I cite that article to illustrate this common interpretation of forces influencing changes in the income distribution.

44. That was a prominent theme in Robert Reich, *The Work of Nations,* for example, and that emphasis often appeared in speeches made while he was secretary of labor during the first term of the Clinton administration.

45. People with different schooling levels often differ in ways other than years of schooling, even if they are in the same age cohort. In 1986, for example, about 75 percent of incarcerated men aged eighteen to thirty-four were high school dropouts even though high school dropouts accounted for only about 23 percent of all eighteen to thirty-four year olds. For twenty-five to thirty-four year olds, who had more time to complete high school, the corresponding dropout figures were 60 percent and 14 percent, respectively. Most of the people involved in crime are young, and the proportion of the populace incarcerated roughly doubled from the late 1970s to the late 1980s. A comparison of the incidence of incarceration shows that in 1993, 12 percent of dropouts aged twenty-five to thirty-four were incarcerated compared with 3 percent for that age group as a whole. Differences in the incidence of incarceration among people with different years of school completed are striking, and differences in earnings among young people reflect not only differences in their years of schooling but also differences in criminal records and many other personal characteristics. The deterioration in their relative wage also overstates the rise in the economic reward that is solely attributable to high school completion. See Richard B. Freeman, "Crime and the Unemployment of Disadvantaged Youths," NBER Working Paper no. 3875, October 1991; and "Why Do So Many Young Americans Commit Crimes and What Might We Do about It?" NBER Working Paper no. 5451, February 1996. See also Jeffrey Grogger, "Market Wages and Youth Crime," NBER Working Paper no. 5983, 1997.

46. Actual (trimmed) mean annual earnings levels in 1996 for the adult full-time workers whose wage trends are analyzed on the basis of CPS data are as follows:

	Men	Women
High school dropout	$19,444	$13,887
High school graduate	$29,287	$19,953
Some college	$34,510	$24,150
College graduate	$44,083	$32,077
Graduate or professional degree	$60,716	$41,653

About the Author

MARVIN H. KOSTERS is a resident scholar and the director of economic policy studies at the American Enterprise Institute. He served as a senior economist to the President's Council of Economic Advisers and at the White House office of the assistant to the president for economic affairs. Mr. Kosters is the coeditor of *Trade and Wages: Leveling Wages Down?* (1994) and is the editor of *The Effects of the Minimum Wage on Employment* (1996), *Personal Saving, Consumption, and Tax Policy* (1992), and *Workers and Their Wages* (1991)—all published by the AEI Press. Mr. Kosters has contributed articles to the *American Economic Review* and *The Public Interest*.

AEI STUDIES ON UNDERSTANDING ECONOMIC INEQUALITY
Marvin H. Kosters, series editor